SEARCHING FOR HER

Searching for HER

A Poetic Journey

MARCUS ARCHER

Right Fit Communications LLC

CONTENTS

DEDICATION
ix

1
GETTING STARTED

~ 1 ~
VISION OF LOVELINESS
5

~ 2 ~
Words of Loveliness
7

~ 3 ~
DISCOVERING BEAUTY
9

~ 4 ~
Words of Beauty
11

~ 5 ~
EARTH ANGEL
13

~ 6 ~
Words for an Angel
15

~ 7 ~
AMAZINGLY GRACEFUL
17

~ 8 ~
Words of Grace
19

~ 9 ~
LATIN QUEEN
21

~ 10 ~
Words for a Queen
23

~ 11 ~
SIMPLY SPECIAL
25

~ 12 ~
Special Words
27

~ 13 ~
POETRY IN MOTION
29

~ 14 ~
Words of a Poet
31

~ 15 ~
ENCHANTRESS AT WORK
33

~ 16 ~
Enchanted Words
35

~ 17 ~
ADORABLY GORGEOUS
37

~ 18 ~
Adoring Words
39

~ 19 ~
DYNAMIC CHARMER
41

~ 20 ~
Charming Words
43

~ 21 ~
RANDOM THOUGHTS
45

~ 22 ~
47

ABOUT THE AUTHOR
51

This work is dedicated to the search for an ideal. It is up to you to decide what that ideal means to you.

This journey is different from my previous book. In these pages, I offer you stories of some imaginary, incredible women. One of these people might just be the one for you. All you need to do in your life is find "HER," the one for you.

As you read, ask yourself, "Who is the one I seek?" Draw that image in your mind, unless you are willing to let life take its course and bring that special person to you without any help from me.

After all, I can only suggest. Enjoy!

Copyright © 2021 by Marcus Archer

All rights reserved. No part of this book may be reproduced in any manner whatsoever without written permission except in the case of brief quotations embodied in critical articles and reviews.

First Printing, 2021

1

CREDITS

DISCLAIMER

This is a work of fiction. Names, characters, businesses, places, events, locales, incidents, and images, including but not limited to sketches and drawings, are either the products of the author's imagination or are used in a fictitious manner. Any resemblance to actual persons, living or dead, or actual events is purely coincidental.

1

GETTING STARTED

MEET AND GREET

You will meet several amazing women in the pages that follow. You will read about who they are and how you could engage them in friendship, and maybe more.

Art courtesy of creativepack
Downloaded from https://www.freepik.com/

Each chapter begins with "Her Story." This will be followed by a selection of poetry relevant to each encounter you may have in the future. These are the "Right Words" that can help you determine what to say. Or you can just use your own words if she is the really the one.

I hope you enjoy the adventure!

~ 1 ~

VISION OF LOVELINESS

WHO IS SHE?

At some point, you look in her eyes and you realize how overly exciting is the look she gives to the world. Of course, you know you are not the only one she is looking at, but you are sure that the look is for you and you alone. You convince yourself that this penetrating gaze is something special that she is fully directed at you.

RFC LLC

Your wild imagination takes you to a special place where the two of you can meet, and you spend the rest of your days thinking of that place, of her, and of the joy of going there. You go through each day needing to see her and to get to know her in so many ways. Your mind is constantly filled with the memory of her, and you want to know more; learn more. You have so many questions that you want answered.

Her soft voice gives you the sensation that she is sharing an intimate secret with you. The words she uses do not really matter, because the melody of how she delivers them fixes your attention on her. You know you could sit and listen to her for days and weeks on end.

Her kindness is compelling. She always has a kind word and a smile in any situation. It is not necessary, but she does it anyway. Her soft voice makes the words even more appealing.

As you listen, you are placed at ease and excited at the same time. What a glorious sensation. You find yourself hopelessly entwined in her spell.

She is easy going but confident. She is relaxed about life but aggressive to pursue that which she decides she wants. When she decides, she is forceful but not rude; determined but not unfeeling.

This amazing woman is a great at listening and at being empathetic to another person. She has a grace and style, and her maturity far exceeds her years.

This real woman's touch cannot be replaced by anything, not even gold. It is a special and unique treasure in indeed.

Who is she? She is one of a kind.

~ 2 ~

WORDS OF LOVELINESS

AT A DISTANCE

Without an actual kiss,
    I can taste your lips
    Without holding you to my chest,
    I can feel your heartbeat
    Without touching your skin,
    I can enjoy your softness
    Without being in a room with you,
    I can enjoy our connection

BUT SHE DOES

She doesn't have to call every day,
    but she does.
    She doesn't have to let me know what she is doing,
    but she does.
    She doesn't have to care about how I am feeling,
    but she does.
    She doesn't have to give me so much of her time,
    but she does.

She doesn't even have to think of my needs before hers,
but she does.
She doesn't have to win my total admiration,
but she does.

A HOME FOR MY HEART

Being with her is energizing,
    She helps my body rest,
    Sleep comes easy,
    Not fatigue when I rise,
    I am regenerated.
So easy to talk with her it is surprising,
    I think clearly,
    The words come easy,
    We share understanding,
    The relationship grows every day.
Every day with her I spend realizing,
    She feels my presence is needed,
    She lets me be part of her world,
    She cares about my thoughts and needs,
    She rejuvenates me.
The thought of a future together is mesmerizing,
    She nurtures my heart,
    She shows me friendship I did not know,
    Her attention massages my ego,
    She is the perfect partner.
In her, I find total happiness and vulnerability.
I find a home for my heart.

~ 3 ~

DISCOVERING BEAUTY

MAGNETIC

RFC LLC

You first saw her on a beautiful Autumn day, and she was running through the park with her dog, having fun. You could not help but notice the grace with which she moved. You watch her from a distance for what seemed like an eternity and then, all of a sudden, she was standing next to you. She smiled.

As you started to talk with her, you understood that this is someone who laughs and sings all day every day with great energy. Her laughter filled the park that first afternoon with great feelings and happiness. It was soon evident that she enjoys life to the fullest because she accepts it as it comes and relishes every challenge. To her, bad news is an opportunity to find a path to happiness.

The combination of her sense of humor and her open, questioning mind draw you to her. You find that she likes old music of all kinds, allowing you to discover art you never even thought of. Every song she shares with you tells another part of her story.

If you really want to know her, you must be consistently aware of her wants and needs. You need to be ready and willing to listen to her words so you can discover her meaning.

With so many of these special qualities, she is also an excellent dancer. She takes every opportunity to dance, whether it is to a song, a commercial, or the hum of the world around her. She is magical and musical in her movements.

What a refreshing way to live one's life! You have never met anyone like this amazing charmer.

Every day is filled with new, wonderful discoveries about this compelling person with the magnetic personality. She will never accept that she cannot do something. She relishes the challenge of life.

Is this the one you should be seeking? So, what does it all mean if you feel the way the poem that follows describes? It means you have found a jewel in nature!

~ 4 ~

WORDS OF BEAUTY

G IN THE PARK
When will my search end?
   The quest for a partner; a friend.
   I searched for someone to put me at ease,
   To experience happiness in every breath that I breathe.
   The day I first saw her with eyes so bright,
   I hoped this was the friend to make the world all right.
   Her eyes sparkled and lit up the room,
   And her smile swept me away like a broom.
   As she passed, she said,
   "My name is G,"
   I was speechless with joy that she noticed me.
   Just as fast,
   She walked away with her beauty and charm.
   It was so hard to catch the electric smile,
   That made my heart warm.
   As I looked around, I could not see her anywhere,
   I searched and searched but she was no longer there.
   Finding her again would be so exciting,
   Being in her presence would be so inviting.

Then one day I sat in the park,
Beautiful day with plenty of light before dark.
In the distance I saw a creature,
Running barefoot in obvious pleasure.
She came closer and it was her; it was G,
And she smiled and sat down with me.
Her eyes were shining bright,
The joy in her face was so right.
Her movements were like a song's great tune,
Her beauty and grace more dazzling than a full moon.
Today, this time, this connection, makes me happy as a lark,
As I revel in my time with G in the park!

NOTE: Reprinted from *The Journey to Growth and Love* **by Marcus Archer.**

THE GRACE OF YOU

So precious is the heart that cares so deeply.
  So inviting are the eyes that watch me so sweetly.
  So exciting is the touch that graces me completely.
  So dynamic is the friendship that grows so freely.
  So amazing is the beauty you display so easily.
  So compelling is your control that keeps me needy.
  So valuable is the love that we share discreetly.

~ 5 ~

EARTH ANGEL

BREATHTAKING

RFC LLC

Her presence forces you to give all your attention and look at the total package. Every time you look at her, you learn something new and wonderful. Just like she commands a room, her lovely personality summons all of your attention, and you are helpless to resist.

Breathtaking in her presence, she walks with a royal air and has an amused, carefree look on her face. She is obviously confident but not aloof.

When she laughs everyone around is drawn to her. She is the kind of woman who could certainly spend time with anyone she chooses. She connects with those around her as if she is not sure she is the star of the show, but she is. THAT is beauty!

You constantly see people giving her compliments. She accepts the compliments but seems to move away from each person who compliments her, moving on to change the subject. is not rude; she smiles and just moves on.

She moves through life with the most infectious smile you have ever seen. Each day with her is a treat when you can look in those dazzling eyes and marvel at those red, full lips. You notice her neck is as smooth as anything you have ever experienced.

But you are not just impressed by her appearance. You come to know that she is at the same time aggressive and shy. She is at the same time powerful and lovely. You imagine holding hands on a walk in the park, knowing that it will be more exciting than almost anything else you could do with her.

Now, you are hooked. Your body and mind are frozen with the anxiety of knowing she could ask anything of you, and you could refuse nothing. Yes, you are mesmerized by the idea that all decisions are hers to make, and all her requests would be yours to satisfy.

Her memory stays in your mind. You joyfully understand that you are hopelessly hooked on this woman.

This captivating woman is more than you could have ever imagined!

~ 6 ~

WORDS FOR AN ANGEL

YOU ARE

You are the pretty pictures I see.
    You are the sexy voice that excites me.
    You are a presence that is sweet in every way.
    You are the one who brightens every day.

WHAT YOU DO

Look at me, and I will gladly look too.
    Smile at me, and to you I will be true.
    Call for me, and quickly I will come to you.
    Dance with me, and you will melt me through and through.

THINK OF ME

If you think of me, would it make you smile?
    If you miss me, would it occupy your mind for a while?
    If you remember our kiss, would more be worth your while?
    Miss you.

THE IDEA OF YOU

The energy of your dance is so exciting,
    The ring of your laugh is so inviting,
    The way you walk is so enticing,
    The gleam in your eyes is so mystifying,
    The totality of you is so inspiring.

SPENDING TIME

I long to be with her,
    Even if only for minutes in time.
    I rejoice at the warmth of her smile,
    I just hope this sweet thing could be mine.
    The memory of her make me tingle,
    Forever occupying my mind.
    We could focus on us and ignore everything,
    We benefit from the happiness this brings,
    The beautiful feelings make our hearts sing,
    We give ourselves without reservations, without strings.
    I surrender all my moments every day,
    Hoping that she will never go away.

~ 7 ~

AMAZINGLY GRACEFUL

ELEGANT

You are not sure you are the one who can reach her, but your mind and your reason cannot hold you back from what your heart sees and feels. This is a person to be known and to be enjoyed. Those facts are clear when you hear her voice, so soft and melodious, saying hello to you as if you are an old friend.

RFC LLC

When she laughs, her whole body moves elegantly. Her eyes sparkle to let you know that what you are witnessing is sincere and unlimited joy. Life is a gift to her and she enjoys every minute of every day. That much is evident in her laughter.

Yes, you have seen her grace and sense of humor, even when someone might disrespect her. Whatever the reason for what might be disrespect, she does not judge people. She simply walks away or changes the subject, whatever she deems to be the best approach to the situation.

What a beautiful thing it is that she does not have an ego that needs to be disrespectful in return. She is never rude in any way. She is always a model of class. You marvel at such power in a woman who is so small in stature. But you come to realize that her heart is huge and that she possesses abundant amounts of elegance and grace.

But so far you have only gazed on her beauty from afar, imagining how great it would be to know her. Her dazzling smile continues to call to you, and you wish she knew how much you admire her. The gleam in her eyes is like a star in the night sky and you are spellbound.

So, you wait for her, anticipating when she will appear. And it makes your heartbeat faster. The anticipation of seeing her is intoxicating and that is a feeling you never get enough of.

You wonder what you could offer this marvelous beauty. You are not sure. But you must figure it out.

All of this runs through your mind, and she does not even know your fascination. Will you tell her? You are inspired by her movements and enriched by her voice. Will you wait for her, or will you tell her?

~ 8 ~

WORDS OF GRACE

CHASING HER

Our first meeting was short and fleeting,
   An eternity passed before our next meeting.
   I thought I would not see her again,
   But I hoped we would be together in the end.
   One day I heard her voice in a room,
   A sign that I needed to see her again, soon.
   Now that we are getting close,
   I have the friend I need the most.

AND YOU ARE THERE

Before I sleep, I need soft kisses so extremely sweet,
   And you are there.
   Before I rise, I need gentle hands to help open my eyes,
   And you are there.
   Before I start my day, your sweet smile sends me on my way,
   And you are there.
   Your presence and beautiful energy move me through each day.

CLOSE

Close is feeling her breath grace my face,
    Close is feeling her heartbeat on my arm,
    Close is seeing the details of color in her eyes,
    Close is sitting with her, watching the night sky.

LOVE HAS ARRIVED

I waited for this day to come,
    To be in your presence once again.
    I anticipated being together as one,
    Enjoying the time we would spend.
    And on that special day I was overcome,
    With an outpouring of love that has no end.

EXPECTATIONS

I wait for you,
    And my patience is rewarded with a sweet smile.
    I listen to you,
    And my attention delivers the light of your eyes.
    I respect you,
    And I can see your appreciation and gratitude rise.
    I adore you,
    And hope our relationship grows as high as the skies.

~ 9 ~

LATIN QUEEN

ELECTRIC

RFC LLC

She is an amazing Latin woman, and she fits any definition of a Latin lover you choose to think of. She is an electric personality: physically attractive, irresistible, with aggressive emotions whether happy or mad. It is remarkable that she can go from hot to cold and back in mere seconds. When she is happy, she will give you her all and you will not have to ask for anything. Conversely, when she is mad she is capable of almost any aggressive act; you just want to stay away at those times.

Whatever her mood, you will never see a boring day with her. If you are with her, you will be living life at high speed in a grand adventure.

As daunting as this seems, this rollercoaster of emotions, it does not push you away. It makes you even more intrigued than when your only notion of her was how beautiful she is. You convince yourself that you can create and nurture all the happiness she can handle. Or at least you want the chance to try.

She is an affectionate person with an electric personality. She is so happy with life that it is remarkable to watch. She has a friendly, sexy stare that can melt you heart. She is kind beyond words.

She is an excellent dancer and who takes every opportunity to dance no matter where it happens. She finds joy in the music and the movements that carry her through the days of her life. When she is moving, she is an art form.

She has an electric smile and a resounding laugh that are both amazing. Spending time with her is an adventure because she constantly explores life and looks for the best in every day. She is optimism at its best.

There is so much to discover as you get to know her. You quickly find out that being with her is a high intensity experience. Everything she does is at full speed because she is determined to get the most out of every encounter, every relationship, every day.

This could be your greatest challenge.

~ 10 ~

WORDS FOR A QUEEN

I SAW YOU

I saw you today for the first time,
  The vision of you is still in my mind.
I saw your soft hands and I wanted so much,
  To let my hands enjoy the first touch.
I saw you today with your eyes aglow,
  This is a person I simply must know.

CHARMED

Her long, sculpted legs carry her effortlessly from here to there,
  She glances back over her shoulder with special flare.
When her hair gets wet, it caresses her face,
  So, the smile coming through her locks lights up the place.
A wink, a grin, a sweet lingering kiss,
  You will never find another woman with talents like this.

IF I COULD TALK

If I could talk, I would say the perfect thing.
    If I could talk, I would ask the right question.
    If I could talk, I would make the promise you seek.
    But I cannot talk, so I wait.

THE SEARCH

A heart that beats to the tune of mine,
    A mind that understands the value of time,
    A personality always focused on being kind,
    A physical presence that is so very divine.
    These are things I value as I search for someone to share this life.

~ 11 ~

SIMPLY SPECIAL

UNIQUE

Her personality and all its features are as deep as the ocean floor, as intense as a summer sun. Being in her presence is a blessing that everyone should have a chance to experience. You know because you are having the good fortune to be in her life in some way. You want this friendship and whatever develops next to endure for a lifetime.

RFC LLC

As you get to know her, you find that she cares very deeply about everything around her. She is compassionate and forgiving in all that she does. Her approach may give you the false impression that she is not confident in herself, but nothing could be further from the truth.

She is confident that she will find a way to be successful regardless of the odds. Yes, she may be feeling down sometimes about the struggle, but you will come to know that she is sure that she will succeed.

She is humble as she experiences life and strives to make the best of it for her and her loved ones. In your opinion, she has an aura of power that she does not fully understand.

She is undaunted in her pursuit of her goals. When she has a bad day, she simply starts over on the next one. She has a relentless drive to succeed that carries her through all her experiences.

You come to understand that she has immense power. The power to impress people, the power to make others happy, and the power to demonstrate how talented she is. When she dances, it is poetry in motion. Positive energy is delivered in her every move.

You enjoy the depth of her personality. She thinks about things deeply as she strives to understand her world and the people in it. She pursues the best in each day with a bold energy that is infectious. Her energy actually rubs off on you when you are around her.

You are, of course, drawn to this star who will not act like a star. You crave her company. You marvel at the gentle look and smile that is always on her face. She is wonderful in that she is the same person in any situation: tired, happy, stressed, excited.

You understand that it is rare that you find someone whose personality is always lovely and so inviting. You come to realize that every moment you spend with her is truly a gift.

~ 12 ~

SPECIAL WORDS

MY LOVE'S CREATION

My love for you creates a fire,
   That only you can put out.
   My love for you creates desire,
   A kind only you and I know about.
   My love for you creates happiness,
   About this I want to shout.
   My love for you creates longing,
   Because it is you I cannot do without.

CONFIDENCE

So many days I walked with you,
   Enjoying the company so much,
   The destination was irrelevant.
   So many nights I talked to you,
   We covered so many subjects,
   And each message was heaven sent.
   When you said you believe in me,
   I could float on air,

Now enormously confident.
When we are together again,
We will shut out the rest of the world,
And my love for you will be evident.

SIMPLE

You are the best part of my day.
    My heart beats faster with each word you say.
    The joy of seeing you just never goes away.

LOVE THOUGHTS

My love for you is as sure as when the sunset comes.
    My love for you is as deep as the ocean floor.
    My love for you is as intense as a summer sun.
    My love for you grows more and more.

RANDOM THOUGHT

My ears are always ready to listen to you,
    This is like hearing a beautiful songbird.
    My eyes need your face to come into view,
    Followed by excitement when your voice is heard.
    My arms wrapped around you is long overdue,
    After a big hug I will consider myself cured.
    Let us make my lips on yours come true,
    And of love's arrival, I give you my word.

~ 13 ~

POETRY IN MOTION

SPECTACULAR

RFC LLC

She is as beautiful at the end of the day as she was at the start. Her movements are a study in grace and her voice echoes in your ears even after you leave her. There is a melody in the way she delivers her words that will convince you that you can listen for hours.

She is not a model by profession, but she should be. Every outfit she wears looks like a designer original on her slender body. She walks as if the high fashion experts follow her lead. Never a hair out of place, never a wrinkle in her clothes, she sets the standard for sophisticated fashion.

She enjoys travel and sightseeing and sunbathing, not necessarily in that order. As you watch her in every setting, like beautiful mountains for instance, you come to realize that the view takes a back seat to her beauty. Every photo taken of her is a masterpiece because she is in it.

The remarkable thing about her is that she is unassuming. She does not seek attention. Her ego is basically nonexistent. Each time you see her, your eyes want more.

Most important of all, she is a kind person who cares deeply for those around her. Even when she is dealing with some personal issue, she can focus attention on another person who is dealing with life challenges.

It is hard to be with her. You are just one of the many men trying to get her attention. One of the many men trying to get her to look their way. One of the many men trying to get her to say hello. This not to say that she is aloof. She has time to talk with anyone and everyone who approaches her.

Her giving personality lets those who are fortunate enough to be her friend know that she cares deeply. She always lets those in her life know that she cares and that she is willing to help. She is truly a blessed personality.

You take every opportunity to be in her presence. You pay attention to her and let her know you enjoy the company. You want to be patient because that is one of her best qualities. You want to create something in common with this natural beauty. Every day you see her you come away more impressed.

Your patience is the key to creating a lasting relationship with her. You proceed carefully and hopefully each time you see her.

~ 14 ~

WORDS OF A POET

PROTECTION

Your warmth replaces the need for a blanket in the cold,
   Your cool beauty drives away the heat,
   Your compelling closeness is like shelter from the rain.
   Your aggressive hugs keep me safe from falling.
   You do it all.
   Your love protects me.

MY DAY

My day begins when she rises,
   Enjoying another chance to be a part of her life.
   My heart starts when she speaks,
   Racing through the day and enjoying the night.
   I get so incredibly happy when she touches me,
   Watching her sleep signals everything is right.

ADORATION

Every time I see you, I want more.
    Every time I hear you, the sound I adore.
    Every time we kiss, my heart soars.

MY HOPES FOR YOU

If you just look into my eyes,
    You will see the reflection of my adoration.
    If you just listen to my voice,
    You will hear the intensity of my dedication.
    If you just hold my hand,
    You will feel a warm sensation.
    If you just hug me tight,
    We will start a lasting flirtation.
    If you promise to be mine,
    We will make a reality of the greatest temptations.

~ 15 ~

ENCHANTRESS AT WORK

DAZZLING

While you were apart for all that time, you kept thinking of her. You were searching your mind for a way to get back to the friendship. As hard as you tried, you could not find some way to get back to her.

Then one day she calls without warning. Things click as if you were never apart and you talk for hours. Afterwards, you remember the glow of her

RFC LLC

eyes. It has so long since you have had a chance to lay your eyes on her. She assures you that she cares about you and wants to try to rekindle the friendship. You tell her you care for her and share that you felt sadness to be out of touch.

The second chance at being with her is better than the first. You want to rush to her place right now, but you wait because you do not want to rush this important meeting. This is quality time that you cherish. When you finally schedule a lunch date, you are ecstatic to see her smile and to hear her laugh like before. You missed this.

She shares with you that she has had some challenging things in her life. She is sorry those things caused a problem between you. She tells you she likes you and wants to be your friend and your confidant, if you want one.

At this point, you are hoping she does not realize how overly excited you are about being with her again. She does not know, though she may sense, that being in her life again and communicating is what you have been hoping for all these days and weeks you were apart.

She says she is willing to hear your deep secrets one day when you feel close enough to her. You laugh inwardly at this because you already feel close enough, but you do not want to ruin this moment when she is sharing her soul with you. You are encouraged that she is taking her time just like you.

Now you have a fresh start with her, so where do you go from here? As you get closer to her, you have an opportunity to tell her how much you really appreciate reconnecting. You take great care to leave the past behind and focus on building something between you for the future.

You realize the great opportunity you have been given to get close to such a dazzling woman.

~ 16 ~

ENCHANTED WORDS

ABSENT

My days are filled with the thought of your presence.
    The desire I have to gaze upon you is so intense.
    I continue you my quest trying to solve your absence.
    The truth is clear.
    If I do not see you, my eyes ache.
    If I do not hear you, my ears burn.
    If I cannot be with you, my heart will pay the cost.
    So, I will be there, waiting for you.

THE PERSON FOR YOU

Think about it.
    What makes the person who is right for you?
    The sound of a voice that matters to you.
    The special look in their eyes that touches you.
    The laugh filling the room that makes you laugh too.
    They belong to the person who enriches you.

IN THE DISTANCE
She is so far away,
But when I hear her voice, I can easily imagine her face.
She is just a memory now,
But the thought of her is a vision of style and grace.
She is gone from our dark starry nights,
But reminiscing about her bright eyes lights up the place.
She is too far to touch,
But my heart feels every day like we are in the same place.
She is too much a mystery,
Nonetheless a dream I must continue to chase.

THE VIEW FROM HERE

From a distance, her bright eyes show gleam.
    From a distance, her smile is more than it seems.
    From of distance, she is a mysterious dream.
    Maybe I should come closer.

~ 17 ~

ADORABLY GORGEOUS

INVITING

RFC LLC

You had seen her before the two of you spoke, but it still took you an exceedingly long time to approach her. When you did, you did not mean to stare, but she commanded all your attention.

She has a presence of quiet beauty, as if she does not accept that her look and her personality are so compelling. There is royalty in the way she walks and in the general way she carries herself. She is carefree but focused; reserved but confident.

Her laugh fills any room when she enters. She is the kind of woman who can occupy your mind and interrupt your thoughts. You are more impressed by her each time you are with her.

Now that you have finally approached her you are starting to learn about all of her gifts. She has a quick wit and an enormous imagination. She approaches every day as if it is the best she has ever had. You notice that she finds happiness in the simplest things in life: a sandwich, some ice cream, a song, the rain, or just meeting a new person. They all make her equally happy and curious to know or experience more.

You imagine enjoying these simplest joys of life with her. You want to learn more with a simple approach too, like walking in the park holding her hand. She is smart and sexy and mysterious all at once, making you more curious and hungrier for knowledge of her with each passing day.

You are ready to give her all your time and attention, but you are not sure that is possible at this time. She seems interested but not connected, enjoying your company but not asking for more.

Her hesitation does not discourage you at this time because you spend a great amount of time with her. Of course, you will be patient. Any hesitation you feel does not matter because you are hooked on her and because you are doing everything in your power so that she will discover this on her own. You want to tell her all you are thinking, but you worry that your feelings might be too strong at this point.

You do not want to jeopardize the friendship you are building. What are going to do to get closer to her?

~ 18 ~

ADORING WORDS

HOLD MY BREATH

The way you move inspires me,
   Floating through the room,
   Humming your own special tune.
The way you laugh enriches me,
   Energizing each and every minute,
   Loving any day with you in it.
Now, I am holding my breath, anticipating the next words you will say.

I SHOULD TELL YOU

I should tell you that I am glad to be with you again.
   I should tell you that I would be so gentle with you if you let me.
   I should tell you that I can deliver the pleasure you seek.
   I should tell you it would be electric if we held each other.
   I should tell you that your whisper makes me weak.

I should tell you all of this, but I cannot summon the words now.

I should tell you; someday I will.

SHE WENT AWAY

She went away today,
    She said it is a short journey,
    But did not say how long we will be apart.
    We did not fight,
    There was no quarrel,
    Our love seemed so strong from the start.
    Somehow, she is changed,
    And she needs answers,
    So, we have a new path to chart.
    She took a piece of me with her,
    So, I hope to see her again,
    Because she is forever connected to my heart.

~ 19 ~

DYNAMIC CHARMER

REFRESHING

When you get your chance to talk, you treat her with great respect. You want to show her how honored you are to share her time. She is someone who deserves your attention. You are encouraged that your talks with her are long, entertaining, and cover a wide range of topics about the world.

RFC LLC

You understand the many great qualities she possesses as she is funny and sexy as well as playful and thoughtful. Being around her is an adventure so you accept the challenge of handling the change in moods that makes her special. This is not a bad change in mood. She can go from playful to sexy in an instant, and she often exhibits other moods in between. It is gloriously like spending time with several women all at once. You marvel at this exciting revelation about her.

She is curious about all things in life. She needs to know not only what something is but why it exists. She is consumed by this need, so she asks questions without end requiring you to keep your attention fully on the conversation. The questions just keep coming.

You do not mind all the questions because she is considerate of your time. She relaxes you in the way she pays attention to you too. When you talk her eyes are fixed on you. You feel an importance in the way she interacts with you.

All of these things have impressed you about this lovely lady from the first time you saw her. As she comes and goes in your days, you are sure she gets prettier every time. Just when you think you have learned all there is, she surprises you with another side of her personality.

When you see her, she always asks "how is your day?" The question is not just a formality. If you do not recount some of the activities you have experienced, she presses you for details. She is genuinely interested in how you are doing and in the experiences of life you have faced.

You come to feel that you have known her all your life. Can you make her feel the same way?

~ 20 ~

CHARMING WORDS

HOPING

My day is filled with thoughts of you,
   As I anticipate our next meeting.
   There is sweetness and energy in all you do,
   Making every day with you worth repeating.
   An inviting smile between us two,
   Always increases the way my heart is beating.
   I hope our connection remains true,
   Because every day it is you I will be needing.

MAKE IT BETTER

You make every day special,
   Thanks to the gift of your personality.
   You make all things fun,
   Thanks to a beauty that all can see.
   You make rainy days better,
   Thanks to your optimistic view.
   You make journey of life great,
   Thanks to the kind things you do.

You make life worth living,
Thanks for being such a wonderful you.

SWEET NIGHT

You and I are so right,
    Meeting without bright lights.
    Candlelit darkness put us in a romantic mood,
    And we relax after eating exotic food.
    So comfortable sitting on the loveseat,
    The warmth between us is so sweet.
    We should not let this feeling get away,
    This is how we can spend every day.

~ 21 ~

RANDOM THOUGHTS

I hope you have discovered much after so many chapters of this journey describing remarkable women and the pursuit of them. I realize, however, that I may not have satisfied all your needs or helped with all of your thoughts or enriched your fantasies.

It is possible that none of my stories so far shine a light one the one YOU are looking for. It is possible that you will not have a use for the poems I have shared.

I say this because there are so many amazing women in the world that I could not have met, or thought about, all of them. I have given you examples of the best women I could think of. Each reminding me of someone I have seen or heard or watched on TV or in movies.

The actual stories I have shared combine one, or two, or more great women into one dazzling personality. But I am sure of the possibility that you might find someone like the women featured in previous chapters.

RFC LLC

So, as you continue your personal search for the one that is right for you, let me offer you some additional poetry. Sharing my words with you may help you find your own words.

I hope my poems would give you some ideas about who you seek and how to approach her. If not, I hope they at least make you happy to read them. Good luck on your search for "HER!"

~ 22 ~

SPENDING TIME

I long to be with her,
  Even if only for minutes in time.
  I rejoice at the warmth of her smile,
  I just hope this sweet thing could be mine.
  The memory of her make me tingle,
  Forever occupying my mind.
  We could focus on us and ignore everything,
  We benefit from the happiness this brings,
  The beautiful feelings make our hearts sing,
  We give ourselves without reservations, without strings.
  I surrender all my moments every day,
  Hoping that she will never go away.

THE SEARCH

A heart that beats to the tune of mine,
  A mind that understands the value of time,
  A personality always focused on being kind,
  A physical presence that is so very divine.
  These are things I value as I search for someone to share this life.

A HOME FOR MY HEART

Being with her is energizing,
    She helps my body rest,
    Sleep comes easy,
    Not fatigue when I rise,
    I am regenerated.
    So easy to talk with her it is surprising,
    I think clearly,
    The words come easy,
    We share understanding,
    The relationship grows every day.
    Every day with her I spend realizing,
    She feels my presence is needed,
    She lets me be part of her world,
    She cares about my thoughts and needs,
    She rejuvenates me.
    The thought of a future together is mesmerizing,
    She nurtures my heart,
    She shows me friendship I did not know,
    Her attention massages my ego,
    She is the perfect partner.
    In her, I find total happiness and vulnerability.
    I find a home for my heart.

SHE WENT AWAY

She went away today,
    She said it is a short journey,
    But did not say how long we will be apart.
    We did not fight,
    There was no quarrel,

Our love seemed so strong from the start.
Somehow, she is changed,
And she needs answers,
So, we have a new path to chart.
She took a piece of me with her,
So, I hope to see her again,
Because she is forever connected to my heart.

THE GRACE OF YOU

So precious is the heart that cares so deeply.
    So inviting are the eyes that watch me so sweetly.
    So exciting is the touch that graces me completely.
    So dynamic is the friendship that grows so freely.
    So amazing is the beauty you display so easily.
    So compelling is your control that keeps me needy.
    So valuable is the love that we share discreetly.

You Are All Things To Me

You are the person I need,
    With a heart that matches mine,
    With a kindness so sublime,
    With eyes that forever shine.
You are happiness indeed,
    With a joy for living so true,
    With a fresh and humorous view,
    With such beauty through and through.
You are a book that I must read,

With knowledge to help me grow,
With vision that will forever glow,
With caring as pure as the snow.

Marcus Archer is a hopeless romantic. He is focused on finding comfort, support, and love from his surroundings. He seeks the warmth that comes from discovering the world and from connecting with another person on a special level.

He wants you to join his journey.

marcus.archer.4U@gmail.com

www.ingramcontent.com/pod-product-compliance
Lightning Source LLC
Chambersburg PA
CBHW070051120526
44589CB00034B/1918